An Ode to Life in Poetry

Antonia Frida

―――――――――――――――――――――

An Ode to Life in Poetry

Vanguard Press

VANGUARD PAPERBACK

© Copyright 2024
Antonia Frida

The right of Antonia Frida to be identified as author of
this work has been asserted by them in accordance with the
Copyright, Designs and Patents Act 1988.

All Rights Reserved

No reproduction, copy or transmission of this publication
may be made without written permission.
No paragraph of this publication may be reproduced,
copied or transmitted save with the written permission of the
publisher, or in accordance with the provisions
of the Copyright Act 1956 (as amended).

Any person who commits any unauthorised act in relation to
this publication may be liable to criminal
prosecution and civil claims for damages.

A CIP catalogue record for this title is
available from the British Library.

ISBN 978 1 83794 154 4

Vanguard Press is an imprint of
Pegasus Elliot Mackenzie Publishers Ltd.
www.pegasuspublishers.com

First Published in 2024

Vanguard Press
Sheraton House Castle Park
Cambridge England

Printed & Bound in Great Britain

This book is dedicated to all the wandering souls, looking for home within themselves. It is for everyone on a journey, for when the road gets rough and we need shelter for our weary hearts, minds and bodies. It is for all of us – this entire human family inhabiting the earth. I'm also dedicating this book to those that have come before us, the long line of ancestors that paved the way and inspired us to be where we are now. And, of course, it is also to all of those souls yet to come who shall one day benefit from the ventures we dared to make today.

I'd like to begin by giving thanks to the both random and absolutely divinely orchestrated circumstances that led us here. It may seem as though life is sometimes taking us on an endless merry-go-round until we awaken to the reality that we are the spinning vortex of innovation, creating our own lives like any artist creates their work of art. Thus, this acknowledgement would not be complete without also sending abundant gracious gratitude to my parents and my family at large. I always felt like my path was never quite normal enough for them to accept, and yet at every twist and turn they've managed to show up in the way that I needed and support my crazy endeavours. I would also like to extend an extra big 'thank you' to Cedric who entered my life at a crucial stage and encouraged me to put myself out there and begin taking the necessary steps to allow my works to meet the public eye. Thank you for believing in me. My dearest friends, especially those of you who also adore poetry and are writing geeks just like me, thank you for sending me your writings and allowing me to send you a poem every time I write one which is practically every day. The essence of play that we have has been paramount to my journey in writing, as it otherwise can tend to become a very lonely sport. Lastly, I'd like to give a big fat thanks to myself for trusting in the journey and continuing to stay the course even when I almost fell off the wagon, multiple times. I am already so proud of myself and am excited to see what else will unravel from here.

Foreword

Beloved reader,

It is with an incredibly happy heart that I offer you this book to read and savor at your own perfect and divine pace. I hope it shall give you as much pleasure to read as it has given me to write or, better yet, even more!

As I write I try to keep in mind and heart that words are merely arrows pointing at something undefinable, grand and beyond the seemingly graspable nature of form, henceforth providing the reader with a sense of limitlessness beyond the words themselves, whilst still remaining in the realms of the relatable, grounded human experience. There are not enough words in the whole universe to express how I truly feel, but as it seems that hasn't stopped me from typing them, and for the first time in a long time I am able to sincerely rejoice at this humble attempt to honor life and the plethora of expansive emotion and experiences it provides us with.

These poems are all compiled from the beginning of 2018 until the end of 2020 as that is when I began writing poems as notes on my phone during my many travels. Before that I would mostly write by hand, causing pages upon pages to have gotten lost in the mountain of writings

I've yet to look through. Meanwhile, these three years have been quite significant in my growth and awakening process as a soul in this life, which you may or may not notice in your reading. Regardless, it should provide ample space for recognition, resonance and deepening in your own soul's journey of unfoldment.

Each poem is a world in itself and I hope you shall discover it with a sense of ease and openness in your being, allowing it to melt you, support you, inspire you, stir the life force in you or put you at ease in times of struggle. Essentially, most poems talk about awakening and the ups and downs of such an experience here on earth as humans.

Writing poetry is my way of essentially holding my own hand through the tribulations of life and, perhaps in your reading them, we are also interlacing our fingers and holding each other through the trials, shedding light onto ourselves and our paths.

Much more need not be said, but merely – please dive in and enjoy this *Ode to Life in Poetry*.

Love-A

JULY 2018

July is the month of the year I was born, so it is natural that each life cycle somehow springs from the peak of summer to me. Summers of heat, summers of rain, no matter what they bring, they hold a special kind of magic that seems to live on forever.

A Good Start

All of a sudden
I ask myself
What is it I'm doing
Whose dream
am I living
I seem to have drifted astray
And forgotten my name
Lost in translation
A sea of promises
Turned into
Shatters
What remains
Is not worth saving
Perhaps this
Is the best place
To start.

To Forge a Path

Your life
Your soul
Resides in
And through your body
In your heart
Are all the answers
To all the questions
You may ever seek
There is nothing
That you are lacking
To be
Who you are
Everything is there
Inside you
Simply waiting
For you to discover it
To explore it
Breathe it into life
It's all up to you
The choice is yours
You may feel it is painful
Remember then
That pain opens us
To truth
To pleasure
To joy
It is an adventure

That once you have opened to it
You can never go back
And neither will you want to
For peace will flood you
Root you to the earth
You'll see again
The simplest truth
That everything is okay
Yet the path must be walked
Forged sometimes
And surely
There will be naysayers
And way-show-ers
Learn to tell the difference
Then remember that all are the same
Teachers and friends on the path
Leading you to the same
And perfect truth
Within yourself
Let everything be that guide
There will be moments when
You'll want to give up
Don't, until you must
And when you do
Pray that God's strength
Carries you through
And know with absolute certainty
That it will
You will have done enough

You will be ready to reap
What has been sown
You will be able to rest again
And you'll catch your breath
In faith and awe
Of the miracle
That is life
That is you
That is the ever unfolding now
Unceasingly.

Obsession

I am
Obsessed with my smaller self
Attached to what I am not
And that which it wishes it were instead
So desperate to be less
than what I truly am
That I would rather die
Than live free
But I am too afraid to die
So with wings of truth
Lended by the strength I lack
I wrap myself around the distortion
Of who I am
Slowly slowly
The lie loosens its grip
In the tight embrace
Of what is true.

Between

I am not a performer
Nor am I even a dancer
I am the dance itself
And everything in between.

Rest

Rest your restless mind
Return to the center
Relax
The world is so much more than it appears
And so much less
You believe you are this
You believe you are that
Let yourself be wrong
Let yourself be free
You are neither this nor that
Wisdom dwells beyond your mind's eye
Release expectation
And be guided by the moment
Be guided from within.

Rise

Rise sister
Rise
It is within you
To rise
You have held on tight for the ride
And now
It's time to rise.

What we Are

Facing every conceivable fear
All
Of my attachments
Dissolving
I give up holding onto pain
I give into love
Purification of the heart and soul
I remember who I am
Why we are
What we are
Pure
Unconditional

Recovery

Heart raw
Bruised
Recovering from
A beating
I'm okay
I'm okay
I'm more than okay
Feeling light
So much light
Shifted
Different
All is well
Saved by my own godly spell
And my unwavering soul's desire
To let go of the false attire
I'm all good
The message has been understood
All is well
All is so so well.

Morning Glory

The glory of awakening to truth
Liberation of the soul
As a full expression
Of the divine.

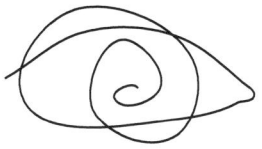

Seeing

Maybe it will burn your eyes
But only for a moment
Before you can see again
That what you feared
Has long gone
And been replaced
By divine grace
So soft and pure
Your desire to run
Has also left
And you cannot remember
Why you ever did want to
What was ever so daunting
When love was always here
Around the corner
Of your jealous skies
Born out of ignorance
Tainted with false imagery
Only stories
Dissolved
Into thin air
Gratitude
Will fill you

To your inexistent brim
For you'll remember
You
Yourself
You have no end
And no beginning
Only as eternal
As eternity itself.

AUGUST

When August hits, it comes with a bittersweet sensation of the nearing of an end. It comes to me as a time to dwell in the bliss of all that has been with the chance to prolong it and enjoy what the last bite of summer may bring before the leaves start turning a different color. Still warm in the late summer sun, we start remembering that everything must eventually come to an end.

Purification

I let love purify my soul
Purify my heart
When life seems to break me
I allow
And I let it
I let myself
Crumble
And the softness of my being
Will be the unmistakable proof
That I am
Unbreakable.

Discipline

Discipline used to be my best friend
It held my hand when I didn't know what to do
Or where to go
Discipline made life easier
At first I hated it
It boxed me in
And then I grew addicted to it
Couldn't feel safe without it
It shut out everything I didn't want
Until it didn't

Until
It shut out more than that
Until I started wondering about these things
I thought I didn't want
And also wanted
Parts of creation
Rejected
By remaining inside a box
Why
When the world is so vast
And
When freedom is within all
And
When life flourishes where all life is welcomed
And embraced?

Diversity
Offers a new dimension to truth
And whilst
Discipline got me from point A to point B
I realized
Life is not linear
And there's more to it than merely getting
There
To the finish line

Most importantly
It's about being here
Now.

When in Doubt

When in doubt
Let go.

Returned to Maker

And so it is
I am
Slowly dying
What once used to be
Me
Now
Beyond recognition
Ready to transcend
Yet another story
A
Forgotten tale
That ran the show
And
Left a bitter taste in my mouth
To be returned to
The ether
Wherever it came from
Fulfilled its mission
And
No longer to be seen
Left and gone away
Goodbye
May it also rejoice
One day
In the discovery
Of its own vibrant
Being
And non being.

Wild Soul

I want to travel
The world again
Discover the depth of my soul
Anew
Dive into ocean I never saw before
Live out dreams I never dared to dream
When did I stop?
When did I stop living for the thrill of life itself?
When did I become too ambitious for my own good?
When did precious moments on an off beaten road with old souls and new acquaintances become less than the most precious thing?
My heart asks
And my head wonders
Am
I ready?
Is this what I truly want?
Or
Am I throwing my life away?
But nothing is there
To be thrown away
Only an infinite now
And a deep desire for love
For life
Adventure
The real
The unforgettable

Riding a train til the morning dawns
In a land unseen
By these hungry eyes
I wish for winter
On a mountain higher than ever before
Sunrise on a green hill
By the rising tide of an ocean
Sleeps in the jungle
Songs in the wild
Excursions in the desert
This life is too precious
To waver in faith
Of true beauty
And love.

Opportunity

Walking into
The wilderness
Unknown
To the mind
Yet deeply felt
By the heart
Surrendering
To a path
Beyond
What is seen
By the limited
Thinking mind
And open
To the endless
To love.

Boundless

Ageless, we are ageless
For there isn't even time
To count the years
We believe we live
We don't live for years
We merely live as much as we are present
Most aren't present even a full year
Of their precious lives
Some are
Some aren't
We count them
As if the years themselves counted
The years don't count
As they are mere bookkeeping
Of how much time
We think ourselves to exist as
To own as ours
Whilst in truth
We are infinite
In both time and space
Merely misunderstanding this reality
As bound by time
As if time were separate
From the timeless divine essence
It is not
We are a part
As it is of us

An idea
That now we abide by
And we believe more in yesterday
More in tomorrow
Than we ever dare in today
But today is the realest
Most honest
Intimate
Taste of time we'll ever get
Of the true creation
In which all is already
Manifest and unmanifest
Liberated
Free
And boundless.

Cry for Nothing

I want to cry
Don't ask me why
The peace seems fleeting
Can it really last?
Just waiting for the next disaster
As if waiting for the next hit
The next high
Like I can't believe
My own ability
To stay centered
In myself
Through the motions
But is it I who is centered?
Or is the center merely
The space where I am no more
Can I truly give up
All attachments
To whom
To what
To me, myself and I
And burn it all in the sacrificial fire
To the God beyond
The eternal
The selfless being
Within every last soul
It is easy for the mind to wonder
Who would be left to speak?

Who would be left to walk
Who would be there at all?
Yet it is not for the mind to know
What the soul already is
That its fleeting life
Is but a mere fraction
A spark
Yet complete reflection
Of the great
Nothingness.

Patience Please

You're still
Awakening
It's normal
You're still addressing parts of yourself
And it is never-ending
That is why it is good
To let go of the goal
Don't bother trying
Too hard
Awakening the whole
All at once
Where's the fun in that
When you can live it
Bit by bit
In every gifted moment
Enjoying the bliss of today
Because
You can't take back
What you've already cleared
It's moved on
As have you
You are new
A different experience
Is birthed in this now
And you can't have
What's not yet here
So have this

This experience
And love it fully
Immerse yourself in it
And
Be the intimate lover
Of your own experience
Bring peace
Into every moment
By letting yourself be
Elated
Turned on by every breath
Every second
Of every day
Meditating on the bliss
Of the simplest things
And learning to love
All the things you've forgotten
Live inside your heart
One breath at a time.

(I'm awake, what now?)

Mirror

Can I share with you
The poetry
That runs
Through my veins
Or must I wait
Until you've come to terms
With who I am
That I am not that
Which your mind
Singles me out to be
Must I prepare you
And first pretend
Like I have any other intention
Than to love you
With all my heart
And with that love
Spill my sacred art
Into every corner
Of existence
Would you run away
If I gave it all away
Or would you see
That hidden beneath
The scruffy blanket
Of these small words

Lies the truth
Like the blood
Pumps through the heart
And the heart
Pumps the blood
That I
And this poem
Are you?

Heart Talk

I center myself
In my ascended being
In service of
The highest good
Unraveling
Unleashing
My sacred wisdom
Recovering
Eternal bliss
And the expanded
Infinite being
Surrendered
I Accept
And I Detach.

Seasons

It started to rain
Maybe symbolic
Of a sadness within
For as an old friend reminded me
We are the weather
And the weather is us
Why condemn the seasons?
Why condemn the clouds?
For they reflect us
Like a perfect mirror
Should we then condemn ourselves
For our tears?
And our feeling?
Is it not part of life itself
To feel?
And experience the fleeting emotion
As the wind that blows in autumn
Full of leaves, life and death
And settles again in spring?
Is it not the glory of living
That not one day is ever exactly like another?
Do we truly wish for an endless summer
Or embrace in the midst of change
That as nothing lasts forever
And anything held onto
Becomes our own prison
And poison

Whether its name be eternal sunshine
summer or spring?
If it is not allowed to pass
Did it ever truly exist?
For it is only in the inner kingdom of God
That such words
ever
Rang true.

Tired

It's time
To turn the tables
All around
It's time
To reveal
The light
Let it pour through the cracks
Of every little corner
And revive the truth
Through the divine soul
Cause I'm tired
Of techniques
And tricks
Of management
And control
To compensate
For lack of trust
For lack of ability to see
I want to live fearlessly
And freely
Cause I'm tired
Of living as if I didn't believe
In my own magic
And the medicine
That flows through these veins
And all its miracles
I'm tired

Of reaching
Where there is no calling of my name
Where spirit is not welcomed
Of preaching
To deaf ears and small minds
Stories way past due
Of trying
Where there is no heart to receive
And no willingness to feel
Of doubting
Where there is a well of abundance
Where love spills onto everything
And brings to life
All that has been forgotten
It's time
To change the narrative
It's time
To reveal
The light.

What you See

For what you see
Is a story
Evolved out of itself
A deep interest
And curiosity
Of the nature
Of creation
Its ins and outs
Its quirks and flaws
How special it is
To be human
And yet absolutely divine
Lost in a sea of living mass
Also infinitely held in the sweetness of nothingness
What you see
Has never lived
Nor has it ever died
Yet here I am
Unwinding and unfolding
Like a frantic yogi
Unknotting himself
Out of the posture
Of his own karma
I am a story
Told to itself
For the sake of playful joy
And so it is
What you see.

Moving Mountains

Oh dear
Your heart
Can move mountains
But first you must come to see
There is no mountain
But the mountain in you
Therefore
As you move
It moves too
For you my dear
Have the world inside you
And as you open
The world is revealed to itself
And that's the art
Of moving mountains.

SEPTEMBER

Come the rain and let the leaves fall, this season shows us the inevitability of all things being impermanent, and yet holds the promise that one day, things do come again with new life and new strength.

Pages

Like the pages of a book
We
Turn to the next.

A Toast to Poetry

A piece of my heart
Cracks open
Just enough
To spill
Into poetry
So go ahead
Lift your glass
To collect my blood
Have a sip
And taste the agony
That made my love
So sweet.

Naked

I have no armor
I am
Naked before you
Shoot away
It will do no harm
It cannot
For my armor is not there to be hurt
And I
As I am
Do not worry of death
Or pain
As I am deathless
Eternal
And unconditionally loving
•

Shoot away
With your loaded guns
No war has ever stopped me
No bullet has ever gotten to me
For I am formless
Timeless
Without any armor
For I am not separate from you
•

So shoot away
And do not worry
Of your actions or inactions

I have been here
From the start
And I will be here
Until the end
And even after
For that is what I am
Beyond time
And beyond space
I have loved you
Since before you existed
And eternities again
I will love
After you've ceased

•

So shoot away
Your guns hold no power
For both you and them
Exist at the mercy of my grace
The source of who you are
Is this love
That I am
Which blinds you
For it is too bright
For your two weary eyes to see
But from the third you'll discover
It is this endless river
Of I am
From
Which you were born

•

Shoot away
Dear one
I am your timeless mother
And father
Wrapped in One
For I am the divine
Within
And all around you
What you shoot at me is the same
The same as what I am
As all comes from me
And inevitably
Returns to me
As I
Its loving source

•

Shoot away
And worry not
About your anger
Or your fear
Or your sadness
It is not yours to keep forever
And I need not be protected
From myself
Therefore I have no armor
I am
Naked before you
As I have nothing to hide

And nothing to show
I am that I am
I am
I.

Playful Heart

Playful playful heart
Were you struck by a lonesome dart?
Did you take refuge
Behind a wall so huge
That now you are unseen
Only to be found in the in-between
Come out come out
Let's go out and about
Let's discover these grounds
And shed those heavy pounds
Of sorrow and grief
Becoming light like a leaf
Flowing mid-air
With not a single care
For you were born to play
In this sacred garden, here to stay.

Ground

A timeline collapses
And I fall back into the earth
I may have been flying
A little higher than my might
Now she holds me as I weep
For I wasn't standing firmly
Enough
Onto the ground
Beneath me
To grow as tall as I was destined
So Mother brings me back
To where I need to be
To the ancient roots of her great tree
To learn about the ways
I used to remember
When I was a child
Young and tender
Free and wild
She called me
Humbled me
With her embrace
And showed me
That I am
Home.

Free Will

Have you favored pain over freedom?
Have you lost your lucidity in the stream of the mundane?
What would it take for you to overlook what you think you know, to see that which you could never explain?
Did you wake up, only to go back to sleep?
Did your head fall so heavy upon your shoulders your body could no longer dance?
What is this noise?
What is this refusal of a love so deep and pure?
Have you not already seen the river flow and bathed in its brilliance?
Have you only tasted freedom to spit it back out?
You strange being
What is this stubbornness to hold onto the past?
Has it not already passed?
Would you rather be gone with the old, or alive with the present, here, now?
The choice is yours, my love.
We are here.
Choose wisely.
You are held.
You are loved.
You are cared for.
We love you.
We live inside you.
We love you.
We love you.
We are you.

The Journey

First there was sheer pain.
Shock.
Then there was sorrow,
deep and imperishable sorrow.
Then there was sadness,
heavy yet mellow.
The there was apathy,
grey and muddy.
Then there was anger and agony.
Pain,
softer this time.
And in between the tears,
occasional smiles.
And then even laughter.
Hugs.
Love.
Yes love.
Light flowing through.
So much light.
Growth.
Perspective.
Relief.
And so,
the wisdom
of the process reveals itself.
Transcendence,
Purity and beauty.
Clarity and trust,
in God within all.

Ready

You thought you'd come farther
And now this wall in front of you
A sign of your defeat
My dear
This is only the sign
That you've got more to unravel
And more to live
Don't worry about getting to the end
What's been put just before you
Is a gift beyond price
Use it to awaken
In this precious now
This wall only hides
What you're now ready
To see
Live
Breathe
And be.

OCTOBER

And so we are beginning to give way for the colorful branches to reveal their innate nakedness and the ground to be damp and cool. A restfulness begins to dawn on us and the summer already feels long gone. There is no doubt that autumn has come and the forest is full of mushrooms and some rejoice at the fresh cool air.

Pardon

Shaking
Like a leaf
Hanging on
Knowing
Its destiny
Can't be a avoided –
Falling.

Choosing Truth

I'm so ready
To never feel like this again
To never set foot in a place where my whole heart does not belong
Because I'm tired
Of seeking acceptance
In the wrong places
When I already know
I have been accepted
By the only one that matters
By myself
As the divine
Tired of returning to these questions
The same that spun in my head years ago
Why am I not like the others?
Why can't I enjoy the same things?
I want to be accepted
Want to play with the cool kids
But all I see is their pain
And their longing for acceptance
Unconsciously seeking
Validation
In every sip of wine
In every interaction
And every toke of a cigarette
My soul aches with them as it remembers
That used to be me

And so it asks again
What is a conversation drowned out in noise?
What is a numbed dance forgotten in a hazy headache?
Distraction
It is all a distraction from the self
A seeking
A needing
A longing
And they call me a seeker
I who have found the greatest love of all
I who hear my own thoughts
Crystal clear as they arise
Because I am learning how to merge with
Dissolve into
The silence that surrounds them
I who seek nothing
I who dwell in the now
Whilst others weep over lost yesterdays
And pine for distant tomorrows
I am the strange one
Who doesn't drink the spirits they hand me
But instead channel the spirit from within
I who know at heart why I have come here
Not because I believed what I was told
But because I learnt to trust my intuition
Yet again and again I make the same mistake
I confuse their pain for my own
I get entangled in parts and roles I have no business in playing

And I lose track of the truth for a moment
I wonder if they ever realize
They're speaking to themselves
That everything is just a game of pretending
A meticulous play
Designed to keep you thinking
That you're only just what you think you are
And that anything more than that
Would be outrageous
Because how could it be
That you are unlimited
When you think you're definitely defined
By the clothes you wear
And the way you made your hair
How much knowledge you've accumulated
To convince yourself you matter
Until the alcohol seeps through your veins
And helps you forget all about it
And for a minute you manage to relinquish
Whatever point you were trying to make
A short lived relief from your own blabbering mind
Only to find it pounding again the next day
Believing even more firmly in the lies of yesterday
I'm sorry that's not me
Because it means I cannot join you
Merely watch by the sidelines
And shine from my innermost truth
The joy of choosing love.

In the Midst of Change

Surely
We are always
In the midst of change
Yet somehow
Sometimes
It is as if we stand on solid ground
But as soon as the roots have grown deep
And the fruits of our labor harvested
New seeds sprinkle the earth
And movement is on the horizon
Surely, I never know what comes next
And when I do
I have merely grasped onto illusion
Like a madman to his hat in the wind
Yes, I forget from time to time
How fickle this existence is
And how it is truly so that nothing ever lasts
But God's eternal beaming,
And should this happen
That I am pulled away from divine truth and bliss
The grounds will rumble beneath my feet
And my fall will be the wake up call
That chaos only happens
To restore the peaceful order
Beyond what I may have thought for myself
For it is God's will
Not mine

That will determine
The course of this life
So may it be
That our wills become one will
That my actions be guided by his loving hand
That my presence be overflowing of his divine fragrance
That my words sound out with his illuminating grace
For I alone am not enough
Merely molded clay
Without God's merciful breath
Infused into his own creation
I am only a shadow of the great beloved
Yet by his word – I am
And so it is
That I submit to the change that is his force
Faithfully and reverently
I die unto myself
To remember eternally
Returning to sacred truth
The eye in the midst of change.

If We Were Seen

If we were all seen
In our essence
Essence would flow from us
Unhindered and free
But some eyes are blind
And when we come into being
In these bodies
Sensitive and raw
We seek to understand
To see ourselves
From the eyes of others
And so it is
That the mirrors we use
To look at ourselves
Are stained
Some more than others
And we fail to see
Just what we are
We fail to see
Who we are
Because we believe
Falsely so
That we are the blind spots
Of those we expected everything from
The falters
Of those we thought would hold us
Unconditionally

We mistake
The holes and the pains
Of the eyes that turned away from us
To be us
And to be the measures
Of our worth
Yet through it all
Our true nature lies untouched
Beneath our misconstrued identities
We come to rediscover
Essence
Pure and simple
Loving
Essence.

Change

I feel it
Tables are turning all around me
Inside me
Change is in the air
It's a new season
But more than that
Everything's coming undone
New
Enters
as
Old falls away.

Sorry

I'm sorry
I tried
To measure myself
Against your glory
To lift myself
Up to your heights
Thinking
I could prove
Somehow
I'm worthy
Forgetting
That love
And worthiness
Cannot be bought
Cannot be achieved
Cannot be created
Outside
Nothing can give
Nothing can take
From what I am
Because my being
Is one with yours
And any foolish attempt
At measuring up to you
Is a losing game
Of trying to be
What you already are.

NOVEMBER

In the northern hemisphere the dark is starting to get to us. Each day the sun sets a little earlier and rises a little later. Maybe some snow will start to fall if we're lucky. Winter is just beginning and some are already waiting for it to end, whilst others are cozying up with a cup of hot cacao and lighting a crackling fire.

Whispers of God in the Wind

I do not grow weary
I do not go blind
I do not tire
Nor do I ever die
And though I am ancient
I never get old
For I am in Presence
The presence that I am
And in this blessed light
All is unwaveringly new
Fresh and forever flowing
And in this blessed light
I am in faithful awe
Of what continues to arise
Unfold
And disappear
Completely in love with all
The high tide
And the low tide
For it is the same to me
In this all-pervading presence
That is what I am
This beautiful
Unending
Now.

Sister

Hey
Sister
Did you realize
We were made
Of the same earth
Under the same sky?
That the same water
Which runs through me
Runs
Also through you?
Did you discover
That the air
You breathe
Is the air
I breathe?
And did you know
I am another you
As you are
Another me?
Seemingly so different
Yet so alike
You and I
Do you feel it?
Hey,
Sister.

Through the Mud

It's easy
It's easy to fall
It never looked so good
But inside
There is mold
And a scent
Which cannot be cloaked
Even by a thousand roses
A bitterness
Always at the tip of the tongue
Loneliness shaped as
Lingering longing
It may look like heaven
But it only shimmers from afar
Inside
There's a rotten smell
Of something
Too old
Too weak
To withstand the touch of truth
And rise

•

It's harder
Way harder to rise
To rise through and beyond
Detach completely
And never to look back

In pain and regret
But only to rise
To grow,
It may look like nothing much
But inside
Inside there is freedom
Something no man can touch
No man can take
For it is given
By the hand of God itself
As the sweet taste of simplicity
Forever fills the heart

•

As the chaos fades
And stillness arises
There is love
Not again
To fall
Not again at all
For love never left
Only ever present
To help
The eternal rising.

Angel

You've fallen
And risen
Many a time
And again
You rise
Gracefully
Taking the lesson
Spreading your wings
Trusting the way
And learning to fly
Again and again
Higher and higher
Set yourself free
And watch yourself soar
This is
Just the beginning.

Rebirth

And so it is true, she has returned
A priestess now lives amongst the modern tribes
And sings songs of ancient lands
East west north south
And beyond
She tells the stories
Of otherworldly stuff
The stuff that make up the stars we see at night
She sings them to life
For all to hear
For all to see
A warrior of love
From ancient timeless lands
The whispers of her ancestors
Guides us home
Awakening from slumber
The new human
True human
That never truly lost their sacred art
But forged a path so pure
For all to hear
For all to see
Of love they say she speaks
Galaxies of light and dark
Of suns and moons
To the waking man of the modern tribes
So we may remember
The ancestors return
And the wisdom lives again.

Choice

Always choose and hold the highest vibration.
Always choose love.
Love always wins.

Message from Gaia

I traveled down to the depth of her being.
Inside her, in the center, she gave me her message,
"Hold me in your heart, and you will know that I hold
you in mine."

Playing Small

Feeling helpless
Like nothing's working
Damn I've done so much
All the right things
One would think
I deserved some relief
A sign
Something
To free me of this struggle
A tug of war
That I can't seem
To do anything about
Out of my hands
Yet it seems
My hands must keep working

I don't know what I'm doing wrong
Resilience they say
But I'm the one who suffers
Must it take so long?
Must the path be so arduous?
Why this relapse
Why this hole that I can't seem to face
Or worse yet
Each time I do
I come out on the same end
Never the change I long for

A mere millimeter
Not more

I ache for better days
In such small ways
That I thought it wouldn't be
Too much to ask
For a break
Perhaps that is my problem
That my longing is too
Minuscule
And in my truest heart
I have bigger yearnings
More worth breathing for
Than the petty mess
I try to rid myself of
Only to get a short respite
From myself

Perhaps this is what needs be done
A grander
More open view
Of what is and what will be
So that I may be free
Of the smallness of my own mind
Its outdated dreams
And dusty structures
Perhaps it isn't the one book
I must toss

But burn
The entire library

Let the wind sweep away
The ashes
And have something new
Completely new
Be born
Out of the empty space
The nothingness
Left by my bedside
As I kiss myself goodnight
Forever.

Fear Not

Never settle for anything but truth.
Slay your illusions with unconditional love and awareness.
Fear not.
Only love is real.

Gift

I will never again be ashamed of my body.
It carries the wisdom of creation.
It was given to me,
Made for me,
As the perfect gift
To carry through my mission in this world.
I am that I am.

Remind Me

I am to be reminded
We are all the same
Never have I
Been separate
From you
Or anybody else
For even as I stand
On my own two feet
They belong to the same
Divine spirit
That moves in you
That moves in all
All of us
We have come
To watch the wonder
Unfold and unfurl
As we are not of this place
Yet undeniably in it
Until the blissful day
We rejoice in our departure
From the flesh and blood
Given to us
As the temporary temple
For the venture
Of our human life
No longer bound
By any earthly means

Diminished
Unto infinite expansion
Back to where it all
Began
In eternal ecstasy
And divine love.

DECEMBER

A month that cometh with a promise of the return of the light, nevertheless not without the deepening into the darkness first. The holidays bring the potential for both destruction and creation in one.

You

Child of God
You who hear the whispers of the wind
As clearly as your mother's heartbeat
Thank you.

Winter Wanderer

Sometimes
When the snow falls
And the ground
Is glacial and crisp
My bare feet long
To wander
Lands
That melt
A frozen soul
Like mine
In the winter.

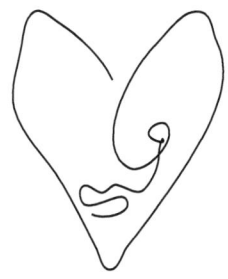

Heart

I'm listening
I don't know why it's so hard to speak
Maybe I'm meant to be silent
Not sure
I'm here if you need me
Don't worry
It's okay
I want to help
I'm worried I'm not doing enough
Don't worry I said
It's okay
There's nothing to do
You are perfect
I'm far from it
Perfect nonetheless
It's okay
It's okay
Goodnight.

Life is the Poet

The poetry of everyday life
Looking out the window
And seeing endless green
A dove silently sat on the roof
Watching
Waiting for nothing.

Eternal

The eternal light shines upon us
From a place deep within
Beyond all thinking

•

May we all come to realize
This place where all things emanate
And the peace that lies here
In the room of the Anahata
Which has no door
No entrance or exit

•

May we all come to realize
That the place we long for the most
Is not a place not a time
But a timeless infinity
Unspeakable
Undefinable

•

May our speech and action
Spring from this well
Of eternal wisdom

Which leaves no man or woman to the wayside
For it sees no difference
No separation
Only Love.

Next to Me

The truth is
I'm
Afraid
I've always been
Afraid
Felt lonely
Like I was destined
To be on the outside
Of everything
Including
Myself
I felt
As if
My own destiny
Wasn't even mine
I've been
Sitting next to
Myself
Not realizing
How close I was
And how I was the one
Separating myself
From myself
Who can blame me
I was young
Not yet ready
To see the fullness

Of my being
And shine
The light
Bestowed upon my soul
I played a
Game
A foolish game
The only one I knew
And now I see
I had tasted fear
And gobbled it down
Like water
As if it would save me
From myself
When all along
It was myself
I was seeking.

Sunflower

A field of sunflowers came to see me.
They told me I am beautiful, that I am just like them.
Face towards the sun, baring and bright.
A field of sunflowers came to greet me.
They told me stories of love and changing seasons.
They told me,
Summer always returns.

Allowing

I've been tested before
And I know enough to know
That this
Is one of those times
A time which requires deep faith
Anchoring the light
In truth
Choosing the highest vibration
In deep acceptance
Unwavering unconditional love
Soul searching determination
Allowing
God
And trusting that all is well.

Because all is well indeed.

Children of the New Earth

We are the soft hearted
We are the warriors
We are the ones without the weapons
Who reach for truth
In the midst of of illusion
We are the humble
Who kneel at the feet of the mother
And stand tall in the presence of our father
We are the ancient ones
Who carry the wisdom of our elders
We are the children
Of a world that our brothers and sisters once dreamt of
We are the keepers of the gates of heaven
Who protect the secrets of the earth
Guardians of the sacred
We are the the future we came to see

Prepare yourselves
And hold steady

For the world will hear us

We are the return of the light
Whom have wandered in the dark
With our bare feet
Kissing the grounds

We are the healers
The medicine
That will soothe our severed spirits
And cure our poisoned bodies

Walk with deep faith
And surrender your mind

We are the bruised and the battered
That heed the call to love
We are the many
And more to come

We are the ones we've been waiting for,

And so it is.

I Bleed with the Full Moon

The return of the cyclical being
The Wombman
Inside her, a living mystery
Unfolding
Always birthing herself into being
Remembering the voices of her foremothers
Learning the art of creation
Of weaving light and dark as one
Crystallizing consciousness
Into a mystical web

Manifestation of the sacred

Purification
Unification
Abundance

Let love flourish
And crack open your chest

Together
We awaken from slumber
In all chambers of the heart

It is the beginning of a new era

We have come to witness
We have come to be
Love.

Let it Be

Let it not be an act
Let it not be a doing
Let it not be something separate from you
Let it be
Let it simply be
Let it pour from your soul as if no one was there to interrupt it
As if no one was there to either make it happen or stop it from happening
Let it be
Let it simply be

Speak from your heart as if the word itself was your heart
Do not worry about making it happen
Be the heart and the heart itself will speak
Let go of identity and you will reveal a river within
which is eternally flowing
Liberated
Reaching the depth
Of the ocean inside you.

Dear Friend

Can I water your flowers
With my tears?
I'd ask for your shoulder
But I'd rather not waste
This sacred water
But that's just my way
Of saying
I need you, but
Please don't look
Be here, but
Not too much
I want to hold onto some illusion
That I haven't fully crumbled
That some parts
Remain intact
Yet I hear
Loud and clear
The echoes of my insanity
Surely the truth resounds louder
For I am crumbling
And whatever remains
Can be left for the birds
For they too
Get hungry in the winter.

2019

JANUARY

A new year comes with the notion of so much opportunity, a chance to do things differently and a bird's eye view of our past. Sometimes this comes with a sense of pressure, other times with relief. In any case it's somewhat of a fresh start, what we make of it is always up to us.

Passing

This is the afterlife
You are dead
Yet fully alive
It's different here
Everything is different now.

If I Could Start all Over Again

If I could start all over again
It would be here
Where my heart
So inexplicably
Finds itself
At home
Surely there must be a reason
Perhaps even many
Yet I am left surrendered
Not knowing why.

A Thing of the Past

Seconds turn into minutes
Minutes to hours
And you get the rest
But in between there's nothing
An invisible glue
Which makes time
A thing of the past.

Faith

Pursue
Pursue what you came here to pursue
And know that you rest in the arms of the lord
In the nothingness that prevails
You are a beam of light traveling through an infinite vastness
Trust your trajectory
You cannot go wrong
You are the creator and the created
You are everything
And nothing at all
Be here fully
All in
With all that you are
In close connectedness to that which isn't
That which is beyond
Know that you are held
And that all is infinitely perfect
Don't deny yourself the life you're here to live
Love it fully
Passionately
Sweetly
Embrace
Embrace yourself
And all shall come undone.

Just Watch

Just watch
Listen
Be with what is
Make love to the moment
It will never happen again
The way it is happening now
In the blink of an eye
All will all be different
So be here
Just as it is
As you are
Now.

Custom Made

A window of opportunity presents itself
You are it
And it is you
Will you discover
What lies beyond?
Will you uncover
The world that you created for yourself?
Every step
A journey
An adventure
Perfectly designed
Just for you.

I Woke Up

I woke up to a new day

So fresh and crisp with potential

I watch it unravel

What is it going to bring?

New adventure

Another song to sing?

I am curious

But I have not gone anywhere

I am still here

Still now

I feel replenished

I am intrigued because I know nothing

The details

Are so lush

And I feel so saturated with awe

Witnessing creation

Living and breathing

Who am I ?

Attentive

Alert yet relaxed

Awake

To a new day.

Ready Made

Sweet surrender
You have my heart
Hold steady
For this I was born and raised
For this I was made ready.

You

You unfold before my eyes
Like a seed unfurling
A river cascading
Making its way
To come completely undone
The sheer miracle
Of witnessing
The human experience.

Like Passing Stories in the Wind

Coming into being
As fast as they dissolve
A flash of light within eternity
Lasting not a moment longer
Than absolutely necessary
For once the hand reaches to grasp it
It has already gone
Like trying to hold onto sand
Or a river flowing
A fool's indulgence
And a child's innocent play
Life's brief moments
Like passing stories in the wind.

The In-Between

Lean into
The in-between
Don't let yourself
Be fooled
To believe
That your life
Is what you fill it with
And foolishly
Disregard
The blessed in-between
Those moments
Suspended
In the air
As if nothing
Was the realest thing
Because nothing
Is the realest thing
You may not see it
You may not own it
Or smell it or touch it
But it is there
Revealing itself
In the precious
In-between.

Love, A

FEBRUARY

We know now that the light does return, yet the winter still has gifts to teach us. Perhaps it is patience, perhaps it is something else entirely. To me, February has that particular feel of something new on the horizon yet still keeps us guessing of what it might be.

Willing

Be willing to die
Be willing to submit
And you will be surprised by the featherbed that meets
you
And that greets you
At the end of the line.

Never Left

I arrived at an ocean of love
Where from
I'd already forgotten
Have I ever left
There I found myself again
But never had I left
The ocean of love.

Watching

Waves crashing
Birds chirping
Light drizzling
Distant thunder
Watch
As the spectacle
Unfolds.

Voice

Listen while you speak
Because you might just have
An important message
For yourself
And through your hearing,
What is spoken
Becomes heard
And only then
Have you truly set your voice free?

Fuel

Unleash the power
Of your broken heart
It was never in vain
That you bled
For the gushing river of red
Only served to nourish
Your own flesh and bones

Proceed with care
And not with caution
Unafraid yet never reckless
You are the one you've been searching for
And you are
The
Omnipresent
Presence.

Try

Fight the urge to write
Deny the right to dance
Close your throat to songs
Unsung forever
It will make no difference
The words are written and unwritten by the gods
You choose no more than an ant
Carrying its weight tenfold upon its shoulders
Relax
You were born to die
But not the way you think
As you are as unborn as your songs are unsung
Only sung by the voiceless
In the silence of the absolute
You believe you know
And therefore you are vain
Naive like the child
Waiting to grow up
You may grow wise
And find innocence in your heart
But even then your soul will be tugged by a longing
Of a depth unbound
A freedom unfound
For it exists not in the realm of your seeking
Nor in your attempts to relinquish illusion
But inside the formless
And outside the form

Where love resides
Eternally
And effortlessly
You are that.

Cancer

You want the cure for cancer?
Then look no further
Than in the density
Of your own beliefs and thoughts

Which seeds have you sown
And water daily
Conscious and unconscious
Observe
The arbitration
Of your own emotional being
What do you allow
And what don't you allow?

Look no further
Than in the depth
Of your own breath
And ask yourself
How much of the spirit
Is welcomed in this body?

There is no fault in your dis-ease
Merely opportunity
To discover a world
Unseen
That you hold yourself back
From uncovering fully

Feed your soul with the silence
Silence of awareness
And truth will emerge
You are as healthy as you are perfect
Impeccable in nature

So return to source
The divine river of love
From which you spring
Let it cleanse you of your illusion
And wake up
Refreshed.

The Knowing

It's a tingle
On the inside
Seems like poison
But ignorance clouds my judgment
For I'm no judge at all
Innocent
Merely looking at the sky
Wordless
Let the venom possess me
Until I am it
And it dissolves
As I too
Dissipate
And blend into the shine of the sun
For truly
There is no distinction to be made
Only a deep
Deep
Sigh of the soul
The soul that knows
It must come completely undone.

Inevitability

The moments don't fly by
They permeate
And integrate themselves
As if
They were somehow
Part
Of me
Already,
Merely born
Out of my presence
Nothing I can do
Or not do
To avoid
Or amplify
Only
Allowing
Yet even this word
Implies somewhat of a choice
Something which
To my ever beating heart
Seems
Like the greatest illusion
Ever made.

Headrest

The world is a place
To be wary of
For those who never rest their heads
So rest your head
Upon your shoulders
Or better yet
Let it sink
Into the loving arms of your heart
Whether in the shape of your beloved
Or your own sweet chest
Rest your head.

Witness

There is no I

Just a witnessing presence

Shhh

You're missing it. Don't look away.

Here. Right here. Everything right here, right now.

Relax. All is well.

Familiar

I've seen your face before
You look familiar
We've danced many dances
And feasted on many meals
Yet the more I see you
The more I come home
To truth
That it was never you
Nor was it ever I
You
Merely
The reminder
Of the nothingness inside
I'm sorry I filled you up to be all that
When all along
You were nothing at all
Words fail
To do this justice
So I fall back into silence
Humbled
Where there is no one
To be even falling
And nowhere to fall
In the first place.

Experiment

I feel like a child all over again
Not knowing what to say
Or who to be
Second guessing
Every move
Figuring out what's okay
And what's not
Observing what's on display
And seeing what's more
Because there's always more
Right?
Mustn't there be more?
Nothing seems
To makes sense to me
Yet here I am
Bundled up
And wrapped in skin
Bone to bone
Moving mass of meat
Who am I?
The torment of having to be someone
When no one
Will do just fine
So I come back
To the zero point
Where none of this
Belongs to me

Yet I am
Everywhere
Glancing through a pair of eyes
Inwardly
Remaining fresh and free.

MARCH

The month my father was born. I know very little about the circumstances of his birth, second child in a German-Jewish household in suburban Stockholm. I bet the air was still fresh and crisp, sunshine beaming through the yet naked trees.

Lying

So you stopped dancing
But I told you
I didn't believe you
Perhaps because
You only danced
A different kind of dance

And I don't know
Who told you
It's bad to cry
Because your uncried tears
Have nothing
But your best
Interest
At heart

They want to show you
What's so beautiful
Inside
Of you
That even if you tried
You could not
Resist
Loving it

And about apologizing
Surely you can

But wouldn't it serve us more
To forgive ourselves
Altogether
Without the remorse

It hangs around your neck
Like a heavy chain
You carry around
For no other reason
Than to remind you
Of things twisted and turned
Broken & burnt
In fear of reliving
What is already
So vivid in your mind's memory
Haunting
Your every breath

Dare I tell you
To smile old lover
For I have done onto you
The same things
You think you have done
Unto me
Therefore there is no need to fight
But simply and plainly
Bury the hatchet
And at last
Come alive

You said you stopped dancing
But I never could
Believe in your lies
So as you speak
Of the devil and his work
I see no more but a last resort
To hide

Yes try to hide
From me
What you never could hide
Because in your eyes
I see you
Ever-dancing

And surely
It is this immortal spirit in you
That I am married to
Without a fault
For nothing
Not ever
Could have me forget
Who you truly
Are.

Premonition

They say times are going to be hard
That challenges lie ahead
That with every other step
There might be a surprise
Something to throw me off
To test me and push me
It will be my job not to be like a rock
But like a river
To flow wherever life takes me
Swiftly twist and turn
Where the path is meant to lead
And let go of any ideas I may have had
Of how and when
And even why
Times they are certainly changing
For that's their natural ways
And with it so shall I
Like a current
Free of restrictions
Going wherever I may be guided
Nothing to hold onto
Nothing to believe in
But the freedom that soars within
And sweeps across so widespread
That every horizon
Becomes home
To the selfless spirit
That moves through me
As me.

Origin

If your read these words
Your calling has been heard
For it is not for nothing
That they were written
And not for nothing
That they found you
You
And your heart
For that is where they came from
From the very start.

No Destination

There is no search
There is no quest
For the eternal
Never left
No time of arrival
No destination to be reached
Only a travel so vast
It knows not where
Nor why
It merely sets itself free
To explore
Its own
Infinite ways
Like the ripples of the ocean
Dances upon the surface
Not to reach anywhere
Neither become anything
But what it already
And effortlessly is.

An Unforeseeable Future

Oh the tickles of life's cheeky twists and turns
Only to spiral back at the beginning, to find

It was never even the beginning
Only the center of a center-less void
An unfamiliar yet familiar place
Where all originates and ends
Where you are and aren't all at once
Not separate from yourself but the same
Like a drop in a sea so incredibly vast
It forgot its own borders
Swimming inside itself
Dissolving
In Love,
Into
An unforeseeable future.

I

There is only the perception of I
The eye is for temporary engagement
For the sake of the play itself
The I itself is not real
It is a peep hole into a show that goes on with or without you
Because the you that you perceive is not the real you
You are beyond it
The watcher looking in

Taking on an experiment merely to have an experience

A wonderful divine playful artistry

To exist as something and yet still be nothing

That is what the I is if anything at all

So do not mistake it as something real

Do not mistake it as your true identity

It is not who you are

Merely who you momentarily experience yourself to be

Watch Perceive Listen

That is how you remember truth

Because the truth lies not in anything seen or heard

But in the seer himself

In the silent listener

He who is far beyond yet ever near

Not part of this world

Yet in it forever watching

With an unwavering wakeful eye

And true eternal love

Forever and always.

Anything at All

If you were told your entire life story
From here til the end
All of it
Right now
It would suck the juice
Out of whatever life you've got left to live
Don't worry so much
About knowing
What tomorrow might bring
Obsessing
Won't get you
To where you think you want to be
Instead
Relax a little bit
And let yourself marvel at the mystery

Know that someone
Or something
Or better yet a no-thing
Beyond your limited mind
Is steering this ship
With utmost precision
And impeccable accuracy
So much so
That no one part
Of the entirety of this vastness
Falls short

Of this perfection

Not you
Not your family or friend
Your dog
Nor the insects you've barely even heard of
Or anyone you've ever met
No one is exempt
From the immaculate nature
Of life
You may call it God
Love or Grace
You may call it by no name at all
It's all the same
To that which it already is

If everything depended
On your worries
The whole world would be in a rut
For have you thought of it all?
Let's hope not
For wouldn't it be a waste
To concern yourself with
Something so magnificent already
So thank God
It isn't your job
To worry about anything at all.

Companion

Tell me
Do I haunt your dreams at night?
Then know that I have come
In peace
To awaken you
From your slumber
Do not shy away from me
However scary I may seem
I will never be
Worse
Than the darkest corner
Of your own dreary mind's thought
So shed light my friend
And you will see
That I am but a mirror
Your faithful companion
On a path
Of liberation.

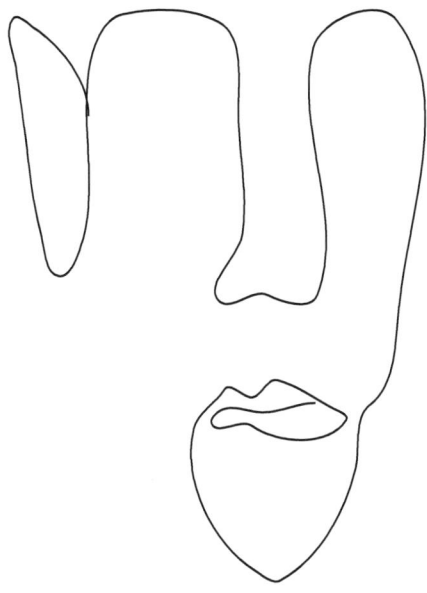

APRIL

Leaning into spring. Most have learnt not to get their hopes up about the weather just yet, however, as the light shines brighter and longer in the northern skies, there is an inevitable sense of hope which fills the air and is inhaled by the long winter-nested creatures. Life is crackling and creeping everywhere, if even in the subtlest ways.

Splinter

The way we are
Is a splinter in time
We matter so much
And not at all
By the eyes of our lovers
We become timeless
We are filled the brim
Overflowing with meaning
True and deep
Where we had none at all
Yet even without them
We are already full
But as stars collide
Souls merge
And our edges are blurred
To remember again
That as much as we are loved
We are that love
Dancing a fool's dance
On an endless field
Of rainbow colored flowers
We live and we die
In no more than a split second
Upon the vast canvas of creation
But we matter so much
That if we knew
We'd burst into new heights

Creating unimaginable galaxies
Only for the sake of play
Only for the sake of indulgence
Of honoring divinity
In heartfelt devotion
Becoming and unbecoming
The awe struck by its own beauty
Like a newborn scientist
Discovering touch
For the first time again and again
Awakening to the reminiscence
For once we have been touched
We must come to realize
We have also touched
And therefore we are one
One with all
And as much as we are loved
We are love

Always and forever.

Writer

"You are the author of your own life,"
They say
But who are you?
Are you not the witness
Inbound by the story
Merely pretending
To be a part of what it knows not to be
How silly
How silly to play one could say
But is that not why we have come here
Each of us
As the same boundless infinity
Relentlessly playing
For the sake of a little fun
A game with no goal
Other than its own
Inherent fulfillment.

Ordinariness

We look for purpose in the mundane
And that is exactly where we find it.

A Flutter in Time

I walked down to the beach
I stopped and drew on the sand
And saw
The face of Lord Ganesha
As I stood back up
A butterfly sat on my tummy
I greeted it and for a moment
As it came to sit in my hand
Admired its delicate beauty
Before it flew away again.

Something Great

I hold myself
Like a brittle flower
In the palm of my own two hands
Soft and sensitive
Is my nature
And though my hands are strong
They are also wise
Thus they know
When to apply firmness
And when to let go
And eventually
It becomes like a dance
And meanwhile within
This flower grows
Into something so beautiful
My hands need not hold it any more
But fall to the wayside
So the new can give way
To something great.

Crystals

Silently speaking
Loving intensely
Without condition
Humble healers.

No Mistake

Make no mistake
You are here
To awaken
Whether or not
It is known to you
You are
Here to awaken
For God's mercy
Leaves no one
Forsaken
Hurry not my friend
The train is here
And you are on it
Whether or not
It is known to you
Your soul's destiny
Will unfold
Accordingly
Cast your worries aside
And let yourself marvel
At the beauty you may find
All along this ride
Make no mistake
You are
Awakening.

Cry

Gråt ut
Gråt ut
Gråt ut din sorg
Låt vindarna vända
Och låt havet storma
Du är älskad
Precis som du är.

~

Cry out
Cry out
Cry out your sorrow
Let the winds change
And the seas storm
You are loved
Just as you are.

In Wonder

I wonder what the great saints feel
When they see their reflection in the mirror
For I am not them
Though they tell me they are me
I wonder
Is it all just the same to them
A reflection in a dream
Faces like any other
Merely hinting at the divinity beyond
Piercing through a subtle smile
Amidst the mundane
In wonder and awe.

Face

Face it
Your face is not the same
The pain doesn't ache the way it used to
And nothing is as loud
As the silence
That resounds
When nothing is left where all would spin around

Take a moment to realize
That you have seen the world through tinted eyes
Behind the fallen masks
An untold tale of heartfelt laughs
The golden arrow
Has struck and said its piece

Will you come home
Once and for all
The good lord knows you've been here all along
And knows it calls you from a deeper place
Giving up the neon lights
You have found the dark has turned to blinding heights

Take take a moment to realize
That what you once saw from tinted eyes
A hall of mirrors broken down
Songs of piercing sounds
To shake you from your slumber

And untie knotted tales and snares

Face it
It's all over
You can go now
Over fields of forgotten tomorrows
Nothing will be missed or done in vain
Living for life
A life beyond the pain
Don't look back just look inside
You've come too far
Not to return
Home
To where you came from
Love.

I'm Starting to See

I'm starting to see
Emerging out of my pain
A world
So blindingly bright
That it rips away
And burns
Anything held
To protect and shield
I'm starting to see
My own naked self
In the beaming rays
Of the divine
To become enamored
With my own form
Like a newborn baby
Held in the vastness
By the arms
Of a father and a mother
So infinitely loving
That their faces
Are embedded
In my own
So that each time
I see myself in the mirror
It is their love I see
Yes,
I'm starting to see.

Ocean of Love

I dive into an ocean
An ocean of love
Not to come out
the way I went in
No
For as soon as I burst
through and beneath
The surface of the water
I have been taken
Not prisoner no
But stripped of myself
Not deprived
Of anything at all
Rather
Enriched, deeply so
For I have become
The ocean itself
As it has swallowed me whole
The I
Is
Eaten alive
Happily so
For once in these waters
One never comes out
A stream here and there
Takes me nowhere but back
Back to the ocean
The ocean of love.

No Matter

Dear child
Whatever you choose
Choose peace inside yourself
For as long as your choices
Are not driven out of pain
Your path
Shall reveal
An exponentially growing
Abundance of love
Choose from your heart
From the most simplistic and bountiful
Spring
Within
For from that space
Nothing arises
Which isn't love
Or isn't for your highest fulfillment
Happiness and joy
In this spectacular
Lifetime
This spectacular
Now
So before you fret
Take a breath
Close your eyes
And look inside
Where are you holding?

Where are you closed?
Now release your clenched fists
Wherever they might be
And try to remember
What were you so worried about?
If everything you ever needed
Was always right here
Right now?

Dress Up

I traveled down
An old and dusty road
Of a past
Tucked away
Inside the corners
Of my closet drawer
Boxes shut
I pulled them out
The pieces of my memory
And wore them
Like jewelry
Had them embellish
My naked form
Who am I
Without them?
Who am I
With them?
I ask these questions
And taste
Their simple answer
Playing dress up
With the forms and shapes
Of who I used to be
Or at least
The chiffons and fabrics
I was once wrapped up
Inside

Falsely believing
Who I was
Had anything to do
With any of it.

Longing

I developed
A longing
True
And deep
To be
With myself
Through
Myself
As myself
And therefore
I am
Now
Awakening
Emerging
Opening
As
Myself
True
And infinite
For all to see
Feel
And behold
The glory
Of who
And what
We all are
To stir this deep longing

In each
For this longing
In but one soul
Is enough
To bring us
All
Home.

Personal

Never take anything
Personally
That's what they say
But what if
It aches
Inside
Like a monster
Trying to claw its way
Out of my heart
What if
Every unsaid word
Unanswered call
Every unread message
Burns like hell
In every
Conceivable
Nook
And cell
What if I'm already
Broken
So bad
That the only way
To heal me
Is to dare myself
To take it
Personally
So that I finally look

Look at the wound
That's been staring me in the face
For as long
As I can recall
What if
The only way
To show myself
Only a tad bit of mercy
Grace and love
Is to take it
Personally
So personally
That finally I see
That what was hiding in me
All along
Were the beautiful songs
And poems
And paintings
And dances
Of this body's
Alive
And preciously
Beating heart.

MAY

There's something so sweet about the month of May, like a drizzle of honey in an otherwise unassuming drink. Suddenly smiles are returning to people's faces and you might even greet each other on the street when out and about. Even the animal kingdom is hopping about and making tracks in the bare ground. Snow is but a memory now, and adventure awaits.

Truth

Some may call me
Stubborn
Others too meek
I am but a reflection
Of what they choose to see
And also that
Which they are blind to
And so it is
Many are the ways
To look upon
That which is
Who I am
But one thing
Rest for certain
I am not
That which can be labeled
I am not
That which can be pinned
I am not
That which can be claimed
For I am the unseen
Living in the world
Of sensory delusion
Here I am
Hidden in plain sight
With many names
And colors to paint me
But never have I ever
Been just that.

Free Falling

Falling free
Complete surrender
I don't know anything
I am.

Eternally Fleeting

Death reminds us that we are temporary
Birth reminds us that we are eternal.

New

I feel tender
I feel sweet
Strong
In a new sense of the word
For I am not fighting
My true nature
Not leaking
Energy
Trying to be
Someone
Or something
Clearly I'm not
You should try it too
Oh the sweet sensation
Steps on the path
Of self-realization
Victories
Big and small
Allowing spirit
Liberation
No longer in a cage
Roaming free
Trusting
Trusting in the true me.

Sometimes

Sometimes
The words come out
And I've yet to know
What it is I'm saying
Am I merely speaking
Out of old habit
Or do I feel
The taste of truth
On my tongue
As they come out?
Like a surprise
To my own ears
I wonder
Was this the making
Of my heart
Or a rehearsed version
Of my mind's stories?
And I lie awake
In the evening
Trying to discern
Right from left
And left from right
But all I find
Is a messy bed
In which I tumble
Can you say
What I have yet

To discover?
Can you reveal
Ever so sweetly
The soft sound of truth
In the golden dawn
Of my sweeping dreams
Humming away
Through the night?
Thank you
To the ocean of wisdom
That birthed me
And the fire of passion
That shapes me
To the breeze
Which moves me
And the earth
That holds me
And shatters me
All at the same time.

Thank you.

Mirror

Has a mirror ever lied
And failed to show you
Or have you just not
Been able to see
That a reflection
Cannot hide
Unless the reflected
Is already in hiding
From itself
And if all that you perceive
Is you
Have I ever not
Merely shown you
Who you truly are?

Knowing

Your lack
Or perceived such
Will grow into a knowing
A source of great learning
Growth
And pleasure
Deepen
Deepen my dear
Here is everything
You once thought
You didn't ever have
But a faint memory
Lost in regret
Make no mistake
It is here
Hidden behind rocks of fear
And mountains of denial
You have come so far
Already ahead and beyond
Rest
Rest in the knowing
That all is
Perfectly
Well.

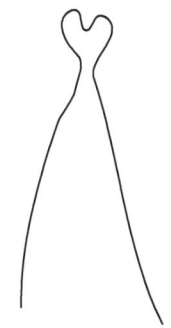

The Road to Home

I am the road that leads to nowhere
Up a hill and down again
You look for me
In all the people you meet
Yet you do not see me as I am
I am there
In every smile
And every heartbreak
I see you
But not nearly as you see yourself
I long for you
But not the way you understand longing
For you understand and see
Only what you believe
What you choose to see
Yes I live in you
But not as you
For I am beyond your limitations, ideas and perceptions
You walk forever to encounter me

Yet I have never left you
I stand by your side
Without ever being separate from you
And you look for me
Even when you don't realize it
But when you do
You laugh at the tremors
And the spiraling ventures
That bring you back home
To where you never left
To me.

Scream

I want to scream
In silence
So that you will hear
What I haven't said aloud
Because I wish
You'd understand
And hear me
Before the deafening
Sound
Of my cries
Am I alone
Or can you hear me
Even when I am silenced
By deadening pain
Inside and out
Oh God
Witness my agony
Before it bursts
For all to see
Or maybe it is so
That you are all the eyes
And ears
I've shunned away from
Forgive me
As I plead
And let this soundless scream
Find its voice

So that never again
It may disturb
The peace
Of the truest
Silence
Which resides
Within.

Zero Gravity

In the infinite universe
Nothing weighs heavier
Than something else
The weight of a bird's flight
Is the same as the cougar's sprint
The touch of a mother's hand
Is the same as the beggars on the streets
There is no in no out
No name is better than another
No job is more noble and no fate is more dissolute
All that is perceived is the dance of divinity
Presenting itself in a multitude of ways
Once you have seen God in one
You shall see God in all.

Words

Words unsaid hurt like fire in my throat
I resist and I fight because I don't know
How they will land
I don't know
What might happen if I speak
So I burn from within
As a martyr for my own safety
But it's all make believe
I have no right to my silence
It's not the kind of silence that carries true sound
But the kind that stops it from running its course
It's the kind that chokes us
Drains us
And corrupts us
It's the silence that kills us from within
The wrong kind of silence
I'm sorry
I'm so so sorry
How wrong I have been
To feed a fire so destructive
Disruptive
Disgusting
I'm sorry
I don't mean any harm
But the heart has to have its way
Or else
It does what it has to do

In ways that may not be so pleasant
Before it combusts
Or withers away
Unsung
Unheard
Unloved
It isn't right
For love not to love
For life not to live
And for songs not to be sung
Words not to be said
I'm sorry
I'm here.

Profanity Prophet

They say I'm
Going to be
A big teacher
One day but
I don't see
What they see
I don't understand
Perhaps
They're mistaken
Taking me
For someone else
What can I say
But the simple
Profanities
That spring from
Nowhere
And end up
At your doorstep.

What is

What comes
What goes
Is not you
And yet
It is all
you.

Yes to my No

Whilst everybody is saying yes
Something in me closes
I feel as though I have to do what others are doing
If they can do it, so can I
If they are doing it, so must I
I get confused
It seems so easy
And good
Like the right thing to do
I've been taught not to trust myself
My ego tricks me and so I must always look beyond
Beyond the corners of my sharp mind
So I second guess and analyze
I'm sorry
I didn't mean to seem rude
Surely I'm the one in pain
I'm always the one in pain
I'm acting out, and you're always right
Here's the narrative
Of you being better than me
Of you always holding something against me
But I don't know who you are
And you may know and see part of me
But have you stopped to truly listen?
Have you given me a chance?
Is it worth finding out
Or will you always know better?

Will you always be the one above me?
Are we ever going to stand on equal grounds?
Will I always just be a rebel
Something unimportant
Someone who stands in the way?
Will I never have anything good to say to you
Because you are better
More evolved
More experienced
More equipped?
I don't even know you
But I tell myself that you must know
You must know better and therefore I have no choice
My choice will always be the lesser one
My choice will always be the one that doesn't quite cut it
But it's okay
I have you to save the day
I have you to tell me where I ache and that I don't need it any more
Surely you're right
I can let go
But what if letting go looks and happens differently than before
What if something's changing
What more must I heal
To say what my heart needs to say
I hold onto more
Doing what I'm told to do
Doing what I'm expected to do

Than when I don't
That is the shift
That is the letting go
Perhaps I see things in a skewed perspective
Perhaps I know not what I speak of

But I must stop and see
What's hiding behind my yeses
Is a resounding no
It's time to take a look
At the layers I've been hiding
Beyond the cover of this book
Deeply buried and forgotten
It's something still alive in me
Yet nearly rotten
I don't want it to go to waste
This part of me
Waiting to come into the light
So patiently
I must trust
That her NO
Is a deeper yes
To a question that has yet to be asked
To a space that has yet to be held

So I ask now
Who are you?
And what is it that you need?
What can I do for you to make you feel safe?

Heard, held, seen and loved?
What have I failed to see?
And how do I make space for you?
Yes
I love you
And I need you
For without you I am not
So come to me
Show me
Let me see you in the light of day
And I will care for you
I will nurture you
I will hold you

I love you
I am you.

Guds dröm

Jag är Guds dröm
En idel drömmare
Inom Guds sömnlösa sömn
Vaknar jag till liv
Av barmhärtighet
Nyfikenhet och glädje
Inför livets oändliga möjligheter
Jag är liksom vinden
Liksom träden
Liksom havet
Och solen själv
Bara en del
Av hela Guds drömrike
En plats där jag får dansa fritt
Den allra vildaste dans
Innan jag åter försvinner
In i intet
Av Guds kärleks bländande ljus
Från dröm och drömmare
Till evig vakenhet.

Kärlek, A

~

God's dream

I am God's dream
A sheer dreamer
Within God's sleepless sleep
I awake to life
From mercy
Curiosity and joy
Out of life's endless possibility
I am like the wind
Like the trees
Like the ocean
And the sun itself
Only a part
Of the kingdom of God's dream
A place where I may dance freely
The wildest of dances
Before I once again disappear
Into the nothingness
Of the blinding light of God's love
From dream and dreamer
To eternal wakefulness.

JUNE

Summer is officially revealing itself and, even though we might still need an extra sweater in the breeze, almost everyone is ready to go out and announce freedom from the rigidity that plagued their souls during the cold months of the year.

New Vision

Learning to see
The world
As it is
Beyond labels
Words
And descriptions
An intimate
Relationship
With the nature
Of reality
Through the experience
Of life
Not separate
From itself.

Losing

"You lost the game
Why are you so happy?"
I'm smiling
Because internally
I'm laughing
At my own deep seated ignorance
At this persistent desire
To always win
As if winning
Anything at all
Besides God's eternal love
Would bring
Any long lasting joy
Any fulfillment whatsoever
That can withstand
The light of truth
And the purity of love's wonder
It is true
I have lost a game
And with it
The lust to win
Anything
But the absolute and immaculate
Everflowing
Love of God.

Break

I had to break
To get back up
With new legs
On solid ground
Before I would shake
In fear and angst
At the slightest quake
Not knowing
If I'd live to see
Another sunrise
Today I have learnt
That my softness
Allows me to move
So as the earth
Shifts and changes
So do I.

A Universe for me

It's not that I'm not scared
Actually
I am
Very scared
But there comes a moment
When one must choose
Will the fear linger on
And decide
Or will one let it subside?

Is there a willingness
To face it
To move through it
And forward
Into a greater unknown
Than the fear itself
Could have ever imagined?

There comes a time
When life will open
Like a flower
And one shall ask themselves
Do I indulge
In losing myself
In its sweet scented nectar
Or do I merely pass by
Without ever truly noticing

How it is so beautifully
Unraveling
Just for me?

Waking to Beauty

I never looked at myself as desirable
Never saw my body as something beautiful
Those who said it were like distant voices
And my eyes had to squint to see their silhouettes
But I was merely pretending
For it had been far too intimidating
To view myself with such awe
And conscious admiration
Of God's own creation
So instead I wore a blindfold
And made myself think
My blood and bones were dry of sacred juice
Devoid of nectar and bland in flavor
On rare occasions I could see
Beams of beauty in the flesh of another
In how they moved and how they breathed
There was something more
Than the gray matter I'd convinced myself
Made up our bodies
Animate and alive
I noticed myself and this body too
To be an extension and reflection
Of what the source within us all
Effortlessly emanates
And so I saw
Beauty.

Perfection

The perfection is not in the opinion of
But in the sheer being itself
It is not for me to question
What has been planted
And placed on this path
By the divine hand
For nothing could have changed it
But God's own will
And it is not for me to say
That this is wrong
And this is right
For who am I
But the mere fantasy
Of that which I truly am
Who created all alike
Only here to serve something
Which cannot be thought
By that which thinks itself to be
Already thoughtless
And only truly felt
Experienced
Surrendered to
And wholeheartedly lived
By that which it simply is.

Little Sisters

I don't seek
To be like you
Inspired
That's all
So forgive me
As I proceed
To love you
As amateurs do.

Slowly Rising

Unworthiness has plagued my broken spirit
For longer than time remembers
But if I am not worthy
Than who can be?
How can I deem another deserving
Of the things I deny myself
Based upon the mere illusion
That I am not you
And you are not me
Eternal one
Wisdom
And holy grace
Remind me of my face
Before it turned the color of regret
Show me my heart
Before it knew of fear
Light up the path
And keep it clear of doubts
Though my mind may fool me
I am willing
Again and again
To serve your inner
True and humble Self
Highest of high
Ignite my passion
As the sacred flames burning within you
So it may burn in me

Your great spirit
One with mine
Amen.

Dreamers

We are all dreamers
Some of us are lucid
Awakened within the dream
Consciously exploring
Navigating our own
Infinite imagination
Others are in deep sleep
Unknowingly wandering
The premises of their own thinking mind
It's time to take a closer look
Delve a little closer to yourself
And find everything you have been looking for.

Plethora

So much still
To reveal
To unearth
To unveil
And discover
Yes
Those are all
Pretty much
The same thing
But slightly
Different
And we
Experience
All of it.

Temple

Finishing what we started
We were never left to despair
Only granted the chance
To be and become
More full
Overflowing
Succulent
Like a plant entrusted an infinite reservoir
Of lushness
And oozing beauty
If you fell to your knees
Not in shame but in humility
Finding the sanctity
Of the holy temple
Inside yourself.

Uluwatu Sky

And the sky softened his deep blue
To signal the dawning of a new day
A migration of clouds
Making its way across the horizon
In shades of pink, blue and gray
We spin our heads in awe
To catch a glimpse of every inch
Of this divine masterpiece
Birds announcing their awakening
As the moon retreats
And the sun reveals his first beams
As if licking the shadows dry from the night's dewy residue
The green becomes green again
And the light returns.

Sit Down

Sit down and have a sip
It may seem simple to you
And simple is not more than I aspire for
I do not need to be extraordinary
For in the ordinary
Lies the divination
As everything that may be
Has come to be
By being an exception
How can we condemn
The blasphemous beauty
Of that which claims to be absolutely nothing
But entirely itself?

The Sky

Healing happens the way a cloud dissolves in the sky
The sky is spacious
The sky does not ask the clouds to dissipate
It simply allows the space for the cloud to happen
To become and to vanish
The sky does not say no, you cannot be here
The sky welcomes whatever comes
Big clouds
Small clouds
They're all welcome in the spaciousness of the sky
The sky does not judge
It lets the winds and the weathers happen as they please
They're not saying go this way or that way
There is simply allowing
A beingness
In the sky
The cloud is welcome for it does not hold the same position forever
It does not come to say I will not go anywhere
It comes to be a part of the movement
Of the fleetingness of all things
To paint the sky in the colors of all creation
The sky is an open hearted canvas
Upon which experiences tell stories as temporary as the wind itself
Sometimes we are the clouds
Unaware of the infinite space we inhabit

Other times we are the sky in the shape of a cloud
Regardless
We are never not the sky.

Afterword

I'd like to end this compilation of poetry with some last words, speaking to the effortlessness with which these words were written. I like to look at these poems as having merely spilled out of me and overflowed onto paper for the sake of love of life itself. It's not something I initially clearly intended but more so something that just happened and for that I am eternally grateful. It's been a learning journey of simply allowing myself to be in my most blissful and joyful state, nevertheless overcoming obstacles and resistances all along.

I am most grateful to all those people that have also inspired these poems and this entire book to happen. Especially lovers across the years that have been my muses, often without their conscious knowledge. Also friends that have encouraged me to keep writing and expressed their longing to read my poetry in book form. I also owe an incredible debt of gratitude to my family who has supported me throughout this life journey and even without their knowing of all my mischief and projects have simply just always been there for me, not expecting me to turn away from my passions and delights of the soul and heart.

This has been a healing journey to say the least, a most fun and adventurous one that I look forward to continuing on as I proceed to witness the unfolding of this book, how it will impact those who read it as well as more books and poetry to come.

Thank you for receiving these words of devotion with an open mind and heart and for letting yourself open to the miracle of life's unfoldment with me. I am in constant awe and astoundment at how things merely flow when we allow, and prioritize our passion, and wish for all readers to experience this pure magnetic force of the heart in one way or another. We are all such abundant sources of essential creativity and we can inspire each other in the most astonishing, beautiful and loving ways.

I give thanks to this life for being my eternal teacher and canvass of playful exploration and art.

Most of these poems talk about the same thing, an unquenchable hunger for the divine within the self and the unceasing awe of life itself. Though the poems often include trials and tribulations, they intentionally do so as a metaphor for how we may overcome these in our full surrender to all that life is – no matter what, and to hold steady onto our truth.

I can already say that a second and even third book is fast on its way and I hope you shall be as delighted to read it as you have possibly been with this one, granted you've delighted at all of course! Either way, thank you for being your unique being in this world and undeniably emanating love at your core, for that is what we all are.

True infinite love,
Antonia